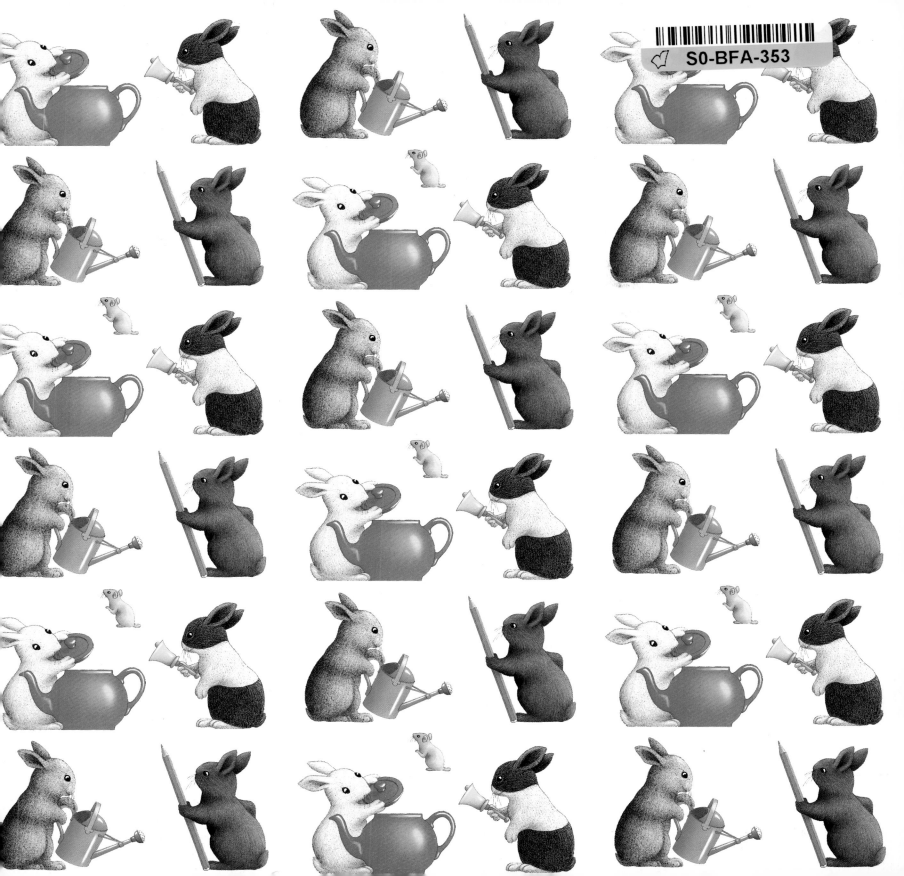

Note to parents

This book contains a wealth of beautiful illustrations showing familiar objects that young children will enjoy identifying.

You will also find numerous opportunities to introduce concepts such as color, shape, and number. You can help to reinforce your child's early learning skills by playing some of the games suggested at the end of each section.

Talking about pictures is an excellent way to help your child develop verbal fluency and a rich vocabulary. By drawing attention to a favorite word, you can help your child confidently recognize words in print. Encourage your child to look at the details in the pictures. This visual skill will be important later for learning to read. Point to and count the objects in the pictures. Help familiarize your child with the shape and sequence of numbers by using the number line at the bottom of the pages in the number section. Point to the numbers in sequence and say them out loud with your child.

Remember—always go at your child's pace and give constant praise. Your help and encouragement will enable your child to make the most of the learning experiences this book has to offer.

KINGFISHER
80 Maiden Lane
New York, New York 10038

First published by Kingfisher as *Little Rabbits' First Word Book* (1996),
Little Rabbits' First Number Book (1998), *Little Rabbits' First Farm Book* (2001),
and *Little Rabbits' First Time Book* (1999)

This edition published in 2001

10 9 8 7 6 5 4 3 2 1

1BDR / 1201 / TWP / *UD CLSN / NYM130/170

Individual titles copyright © Alan Baker 1996, 1998, 1999, 2001
Little Rabbits' First Number Book text copyright © Kate Petty 1998
This edition copyright © Alan Baker and Kate Petty 2001
All rights reserved under International and Pan-American Copyright Conventions

LIBRARY OF CONGRESS CATALOGING-IN-PUBLICATION DATA
has been applied for.

ISBN 0-7534-5549-8

Printed in Singapore

Little Rabbits' First Word Book

Clothes

shoes

cap

socks

buttons

jacket

shirt

underpants

sweater

dress

pants

vest

rain
boots

In the kitchen

cup

plate

saucer

teapot

mug

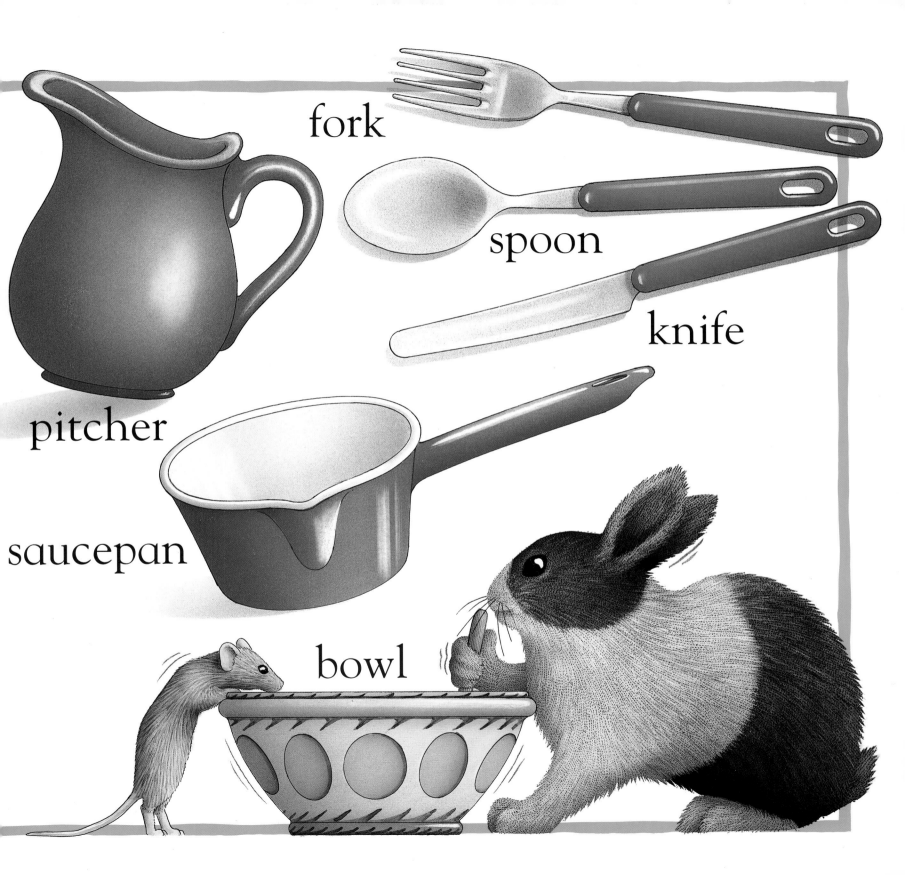

fork

spoon

knife

pitcher

saucepan

bowl

Toys

telephone

doll

wagon

blocks

rattle

puzzle

beads

cards

train

Animals

giraffe

elephant

parrot

tiger

monkey

crocodile

kangaroo

lion

panda

zebra

snake

Around the house

books

cushion

keys

dustpan

brush

broom

picture

lamp

vase

table

chair

In the garden

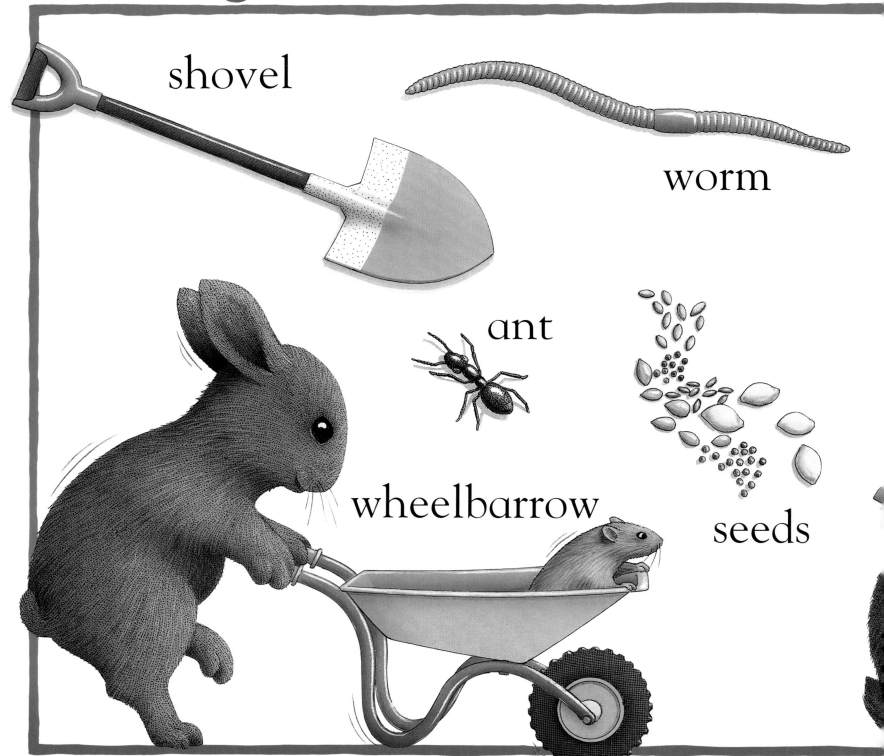

shovel

worm

ant

seeds

wheelbarrow

flower

flowerpot

leaf

watering can

rake

Making a noise

whistle

recorder

drum

flute

tambourine

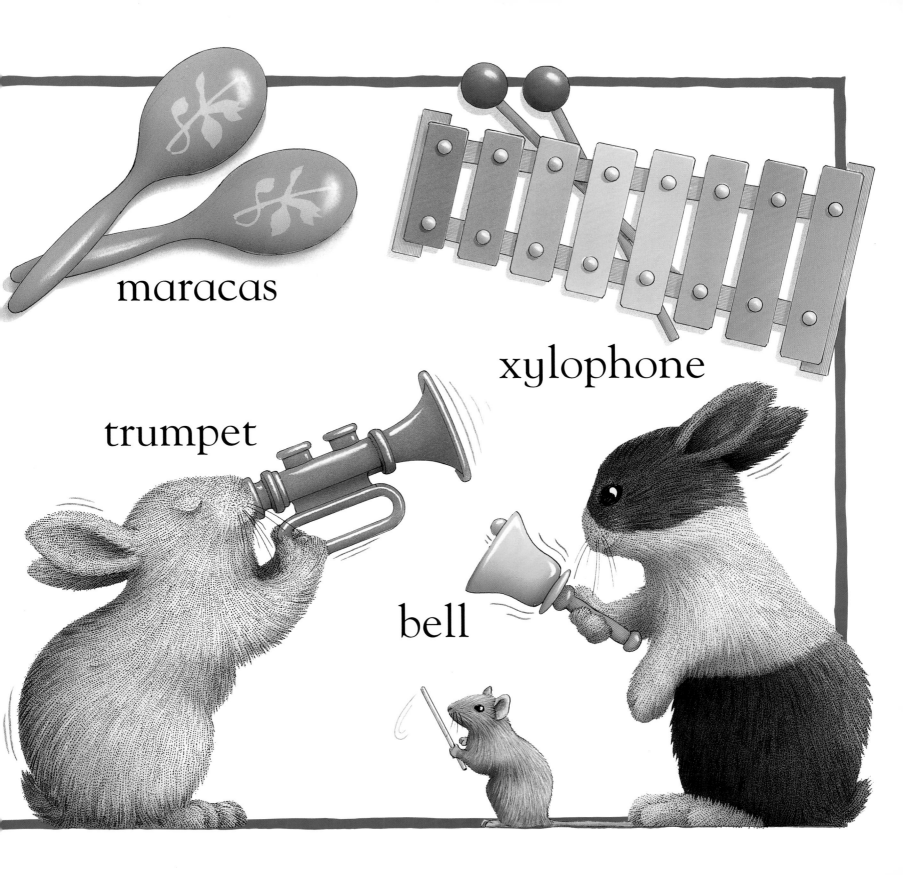

maracas

xylophone

trumpet

bell

Drawing and painting

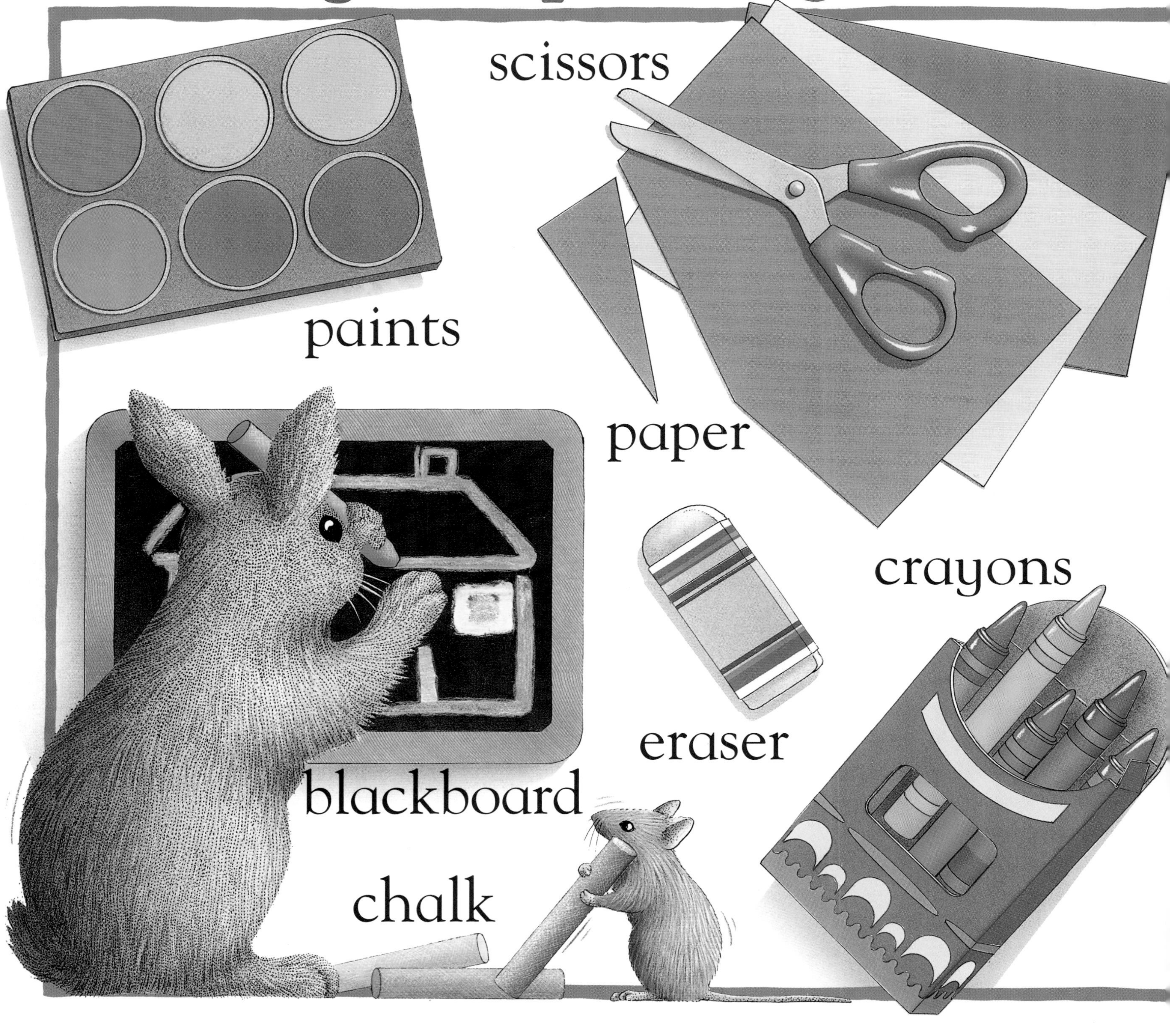

scissors

paints

paper

crayons

blackboard

eraser

chalk

ruler

felt-tip pens

paintbrushes

pencil

easel

Colors

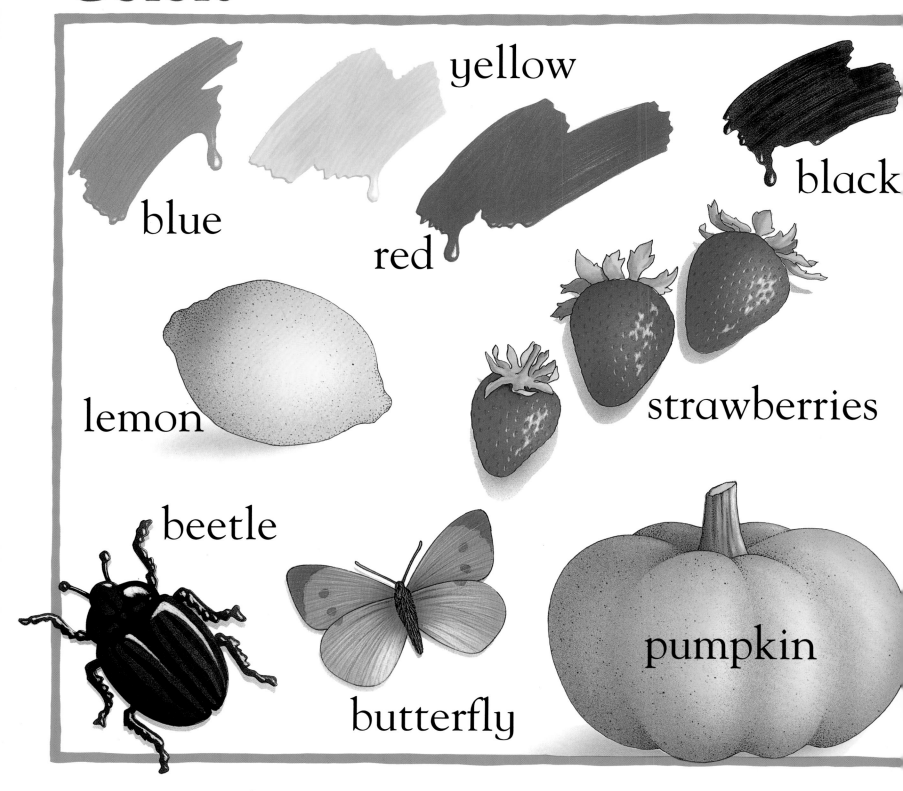

blue

yellow

red

black

lemon

strawberries

beetle

butterfly

pumpkin

purple

brown

green

orange

rabbit

frog

grapes

Shapes

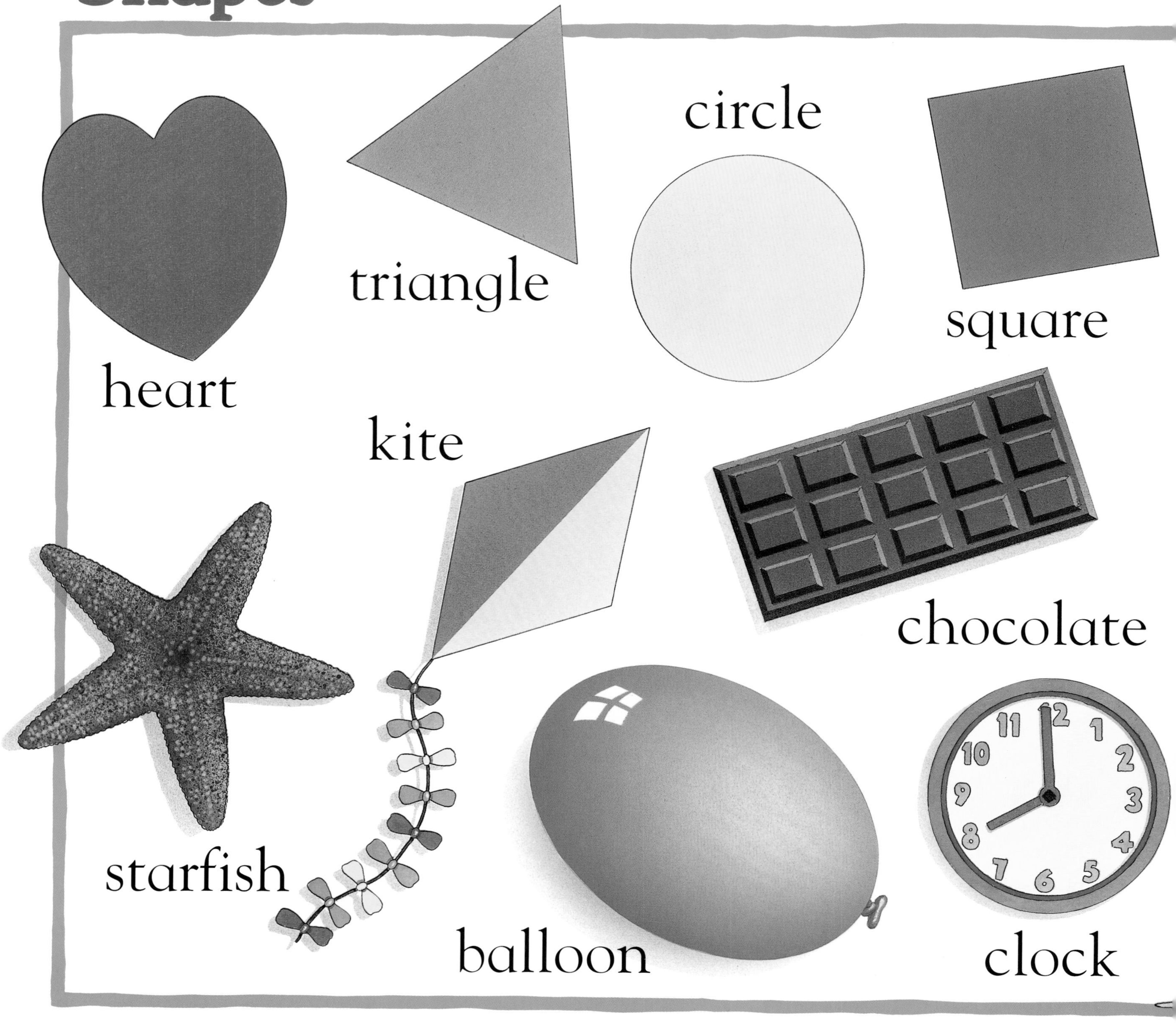

heart

triangle

circle

square

kite

chocolate

starfish

balloon

clock

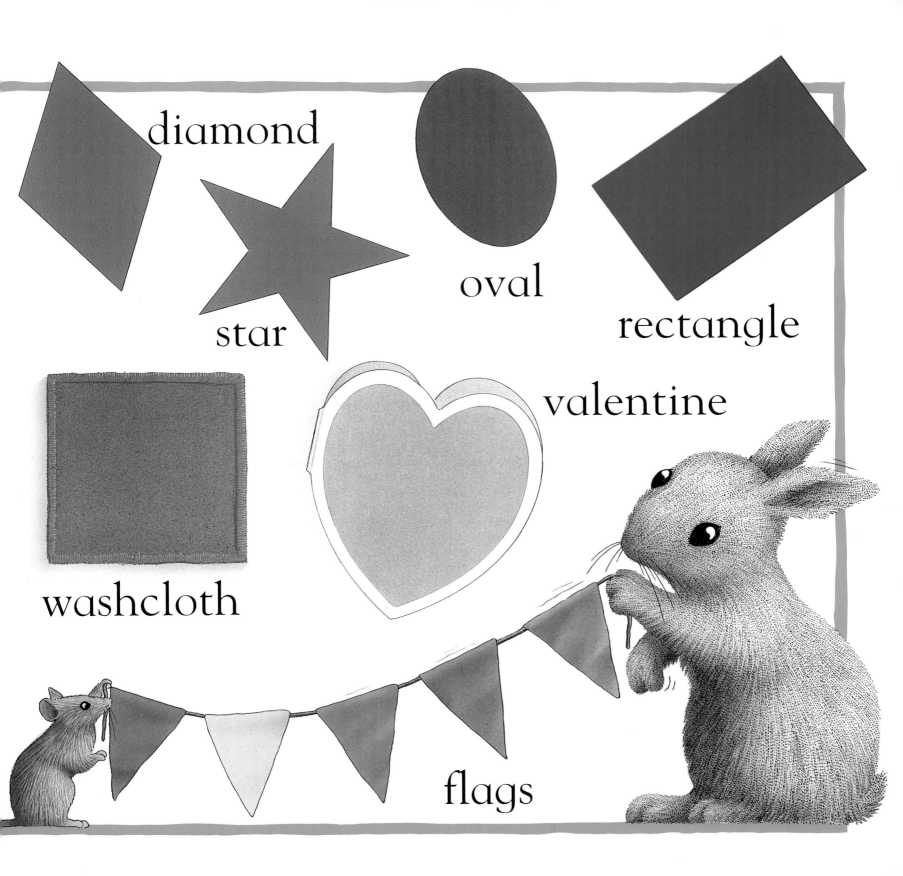

diamond

star

oval

rectangle

valentine

washcloth

flags

At the park

umbrella

swing

bench

bicycle

tree

slide

seesaw

Things to eat

cookies

sandwich

apple

banana

cheese

carrots

orange

noodles

corn

tomato

yogurt

lettuce

ice cream

On the farm

pig

chicks

horse

cow

goat

dog

duck

rooster

hen

sheep

tractor

Bathtime

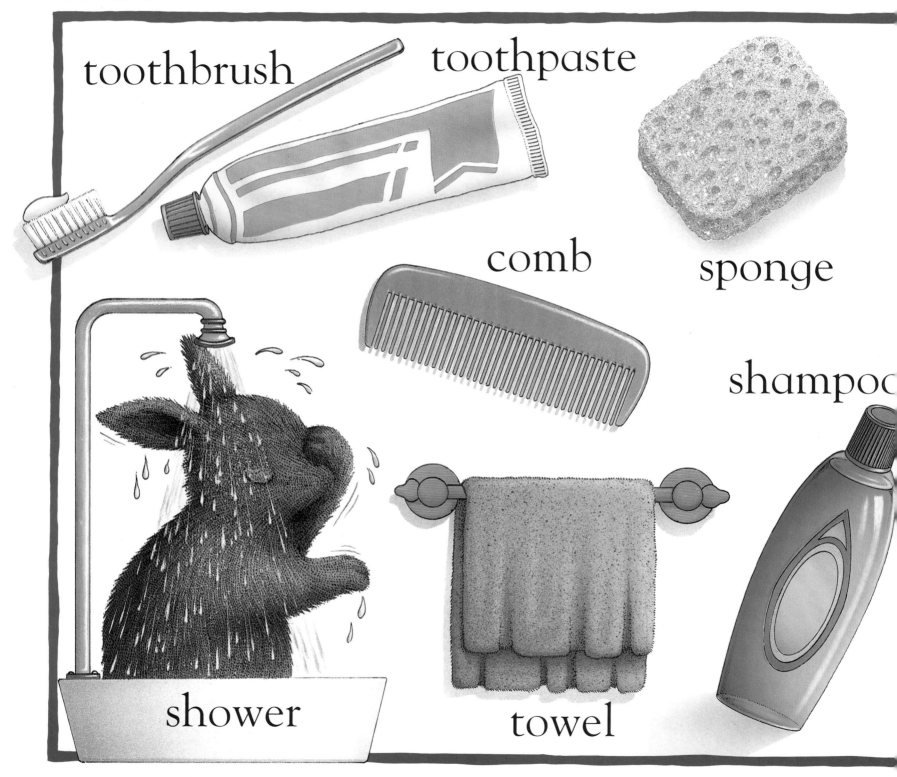

toothbrush

toothpaste

sponge

comb

shampoo

shower

towel

hairbrush

bubbles

soap

talcum
powder

mirror

bathtub

Bedtime

quilt

slippers

bathrobe

blanket

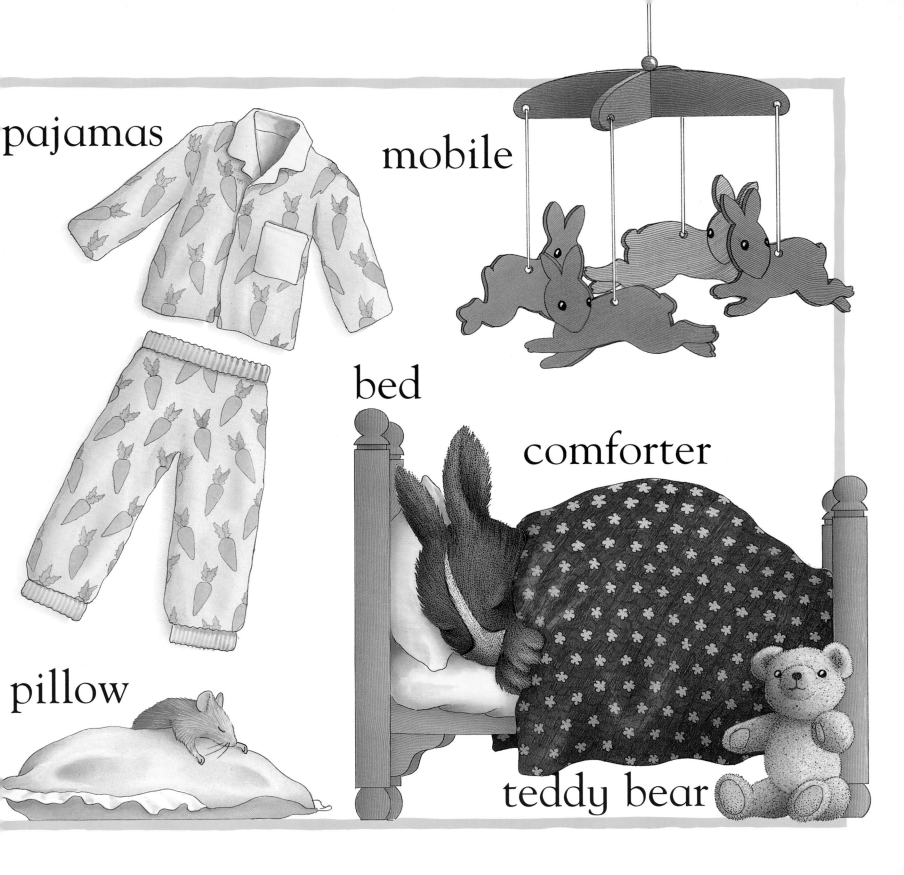

pajamas

mobile

bed

comforter

pillow

teddy bear

Games to play

Playing these games with your child makes learning to recognize colors and shapes more fun. They will help develop observation as well as verbal, sorting, and matching skills.

Where's the mouse?

Ask your child to look for the little brown mouse that appears in every scene. Help him or her to describe what the mouse is doing.

Who says moo?

Very young children love identifying and imitating animal noises. See if your child can find the animal to match the noises you make. Alternatively, point to an animal and ask your child to make the right noise.

Color match

Ask your child to say what is blue on the color pages. Continue through the other six colors, matching each brushstroke to the fruit or animal of the same color.

Shape match

Help your child to find an object to match each of the two-dimensional shapes shown at the top of the shape pages. Introduce the names of some of the shapes.

What is round?

Help your child to look for round shapes or circles on some pages. Examples are: buttons, plate, beads, train wheels, tambourine, paint box colors, circle and clock, wheels, and bubbles.

Big and little

Ask your child which is the biggest animal and which is the smallest on the animal pages. Extend the discussion to other characteristics, for example: Who can fly? Who has stripes? Who can jump?

Match the words and pictures.

ant
ball
cushion
drum
fork
hairbrush
kite
leaf
orange
paints
pitcher
shoes
telephone
worm
yogurt

Little Rabbits' First Number Book

Count to ten

1 one bear

2 two slippers

3 three ducks

6 six blocks

7 seven cookies

1 **2** **3** **4** **5**

4 four hats

5 five presents

8 eight strawberries

9 nine books

10 ten bubbles

6 7 8 9 10

Count the animals

Help Black and White Rabbit find . . .

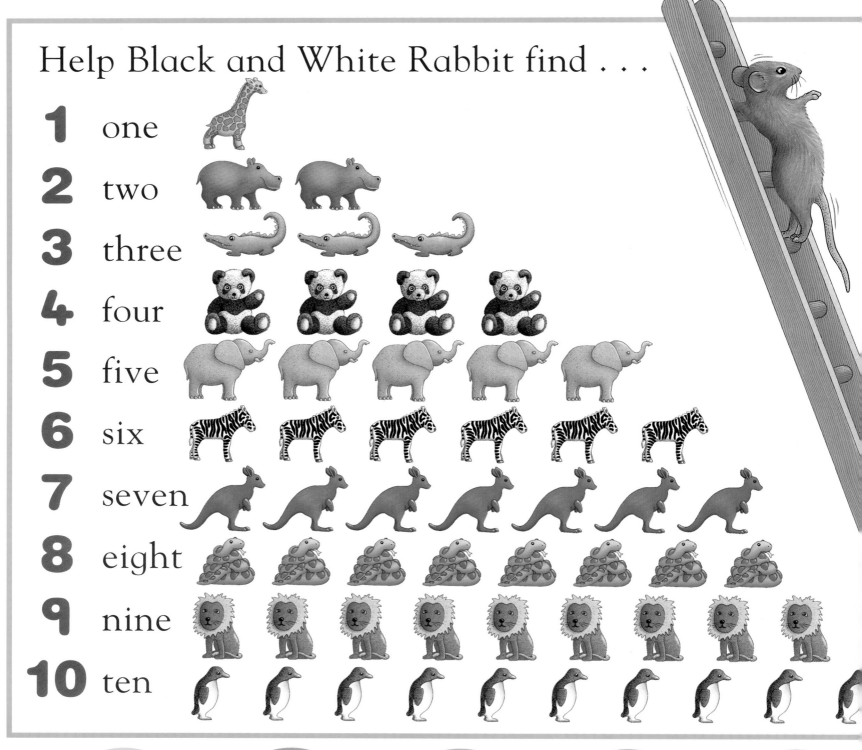

1 one

2 two

3 three

4 four

5 five

6 six

7 seven

8 eight

9 nine

10 ten

1 2 3 4 5

6　　7　　8　　9　　10

How many wheels?

What has . . .

1 wheel? **2** wheels? **3** wheels?

4 wheels? **6** wheels?

8 wheels?

1 **2** **3** **4** **5**

Is there anything that has no wheels?

6　7　8　9　10

Boats on the water

Count the boats with red sails.
Count the boats with yellow sails.
Can you find a boat with no sails?

1 2 3 4 5

How many boats have flags?

6   7   8   9   10

What does ten look like?

Ten of everything!
Use your fingers to help you count.

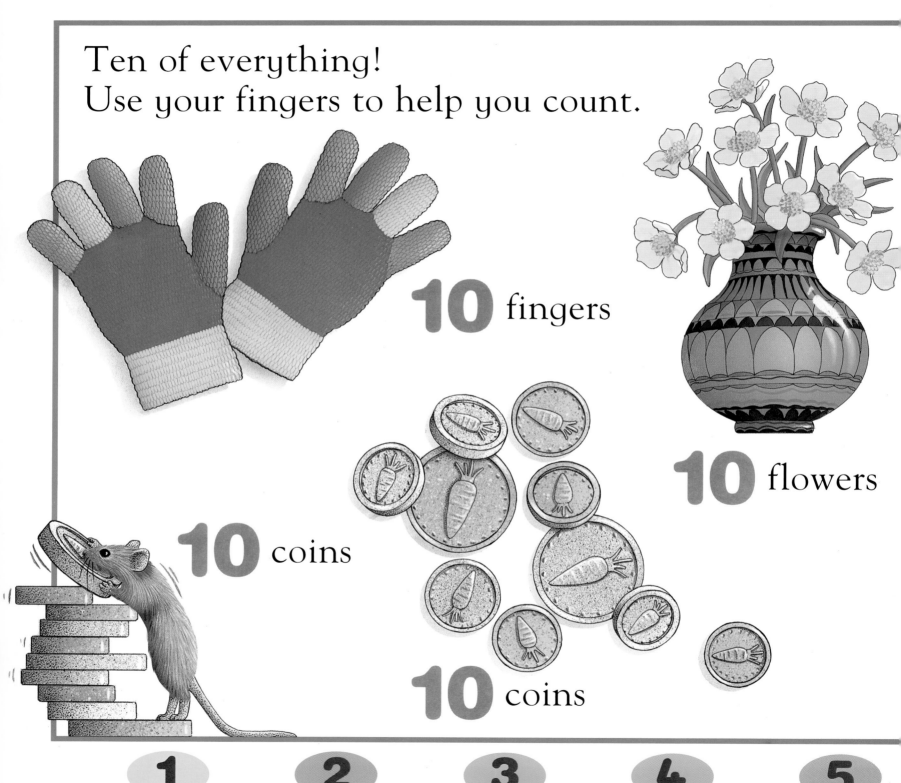

10 fingers

10 flowers

10 coins

10 coins

1 2 3 4 5

10 flowers

10 candies

10 candies

10 blocks

10 blocks

6 7 8 9 10

Happy Birthday!

It's White Rabbit's birthday!
How old is she?

How many rabbits have come to her party?

How many balloons are there?
Can each rabbit take one home?

Is there a party
bag for everyone
at the party?

Here comes Mouse
with the juice.
Is there a glass for
everybody?

6   7   8   9   10

Shopping

Gray Rabbit is shopping for his favorite food.

Carrots 8¢ each

Onions 6¢ each

Potatoes 2¢ each

Tomatoes 7¢ each

1 2 3 4 5

He brings along his allowance.

How much does each carrot cost?

How many carrots are in his basket?

How many bills is he giving to Brown Rabbit?

6　　**7**　　**8**　　**9**　　**10**

Who has the most?

Which butterfly has the most spots?

Which rabbit has the fewest strawberries?

Does the red flower have fewer petals than the other flowers?

Does the centipede have more legs than the other creepy-crawlies?

Look who has eaten too much!

Pairs

Help White Rabbit match the pairs of socks.
How many pairs of socks are there?

1 2 3 4 5

How many pairs of shoes are there?
Can you see Mouse's other shoe?

6 7 8 9 10

Winning numbers

1st Which car is first?

2nd Which car is second?

3rd Which car is third?

1 2 3 4 5

And can you see who is last?

Finish

6 7 8 9 10

What comes after ten?

Gray Rabbit and Black and White Rabbit
are building tall towers.
What shape is on the tenth block?
Can you count all the way up to twenty?

fifteen
15

fourteen
14

thirteen
13

twelve
12

eleven
11

11 12 13 14 15

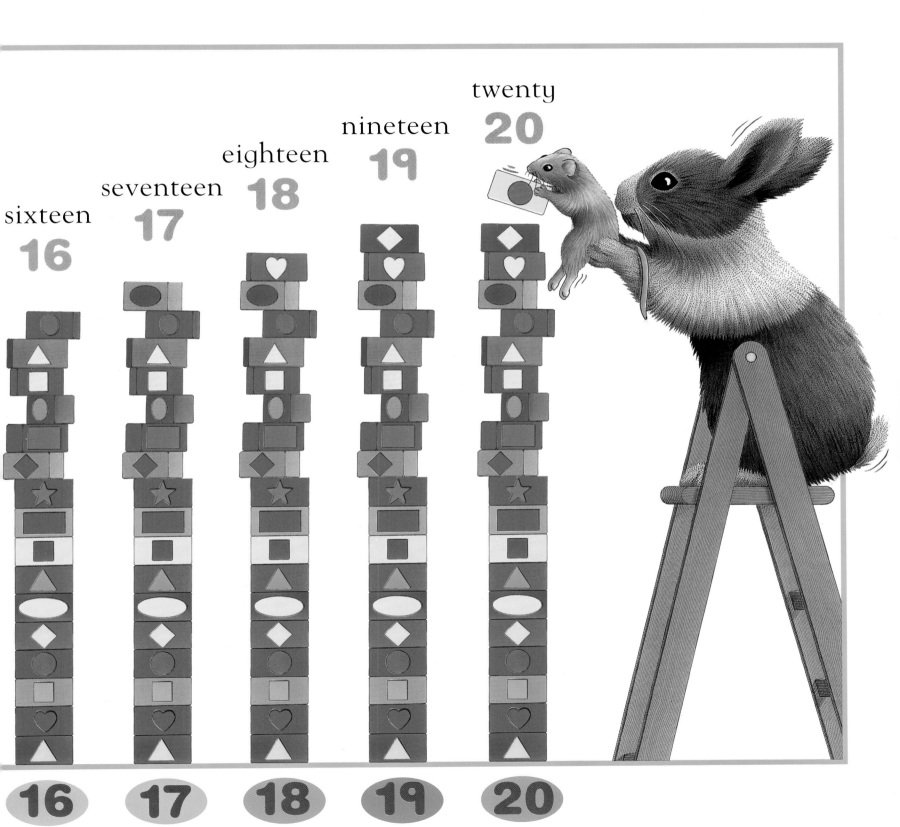

sixteen
16

seventeen
17

eighteen
18

nineteen
19

twenty
20

16 17 18 19 20

More games to play

Playing games will further increase your child's confidence in using numbers. Here are some games to play with this book, plus ideas for playing with numbers in everyday life.

Giant number line

Draw the numbers 1 to 10 on paper plates. Mix up the plates, then help your child put them in order. Lay the plates in a sequential pattern (like hopscotch) on the floor so that your child can hop—literally—from one number to the next!

Mouse count

Ask your child to look for the little brown mouse that appears throughout the book. Count how many times Mouse appears. You can do the same with each of the rabbits. How many different rabbits are there?

Sort the socks

Ask your child to look again at White Rabbit's socks on pages 22 and 23. How many striped socks are there? How many with yellow on them? Play this game with real clothing, and talk about the different ways to sort—by type of clothing, by color, by pattern, etc.

Perfect pairs

Discuss things that come in pairs, such as 2 eyes, 2 ears, 2 hands, 2 feet. What else comes in twos?

Tiny shopper

Use real groceries for counting practice. Young children often find it easier to count real objects instead of pictures on a page. Your child can count the items in your shopping cart or play simple sorting games, such as putting cans into one pile and boxes into another. You can introduce the concept of money by using objects such as buttons or raisins as pretend coins.

Big numbers, favorite numbers

Children love words that roll off the tongue. You can encourage your child to play with numbers in this way, too. Ask your child to think up a **really** big number. Even if it is nonsensical like "ninety-twenty-thousand-hundred," you can talk about it to help your child understand the order of bigger numbers—thousands are bigger than hundreds, for example.

Numbers everywhere

Look out for numbers in the world around you—and help your child to enjoy applying their newly found number skills.

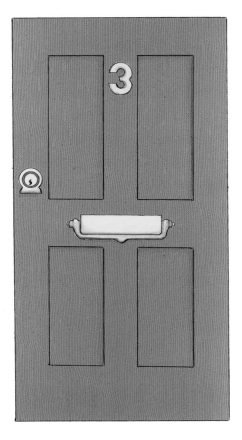

Little Rabbits'
First Farm Book

Wake up, farm!

It's early in the morning, and the Little Rabbits have come to help on the farm.
The rooster is crowing.

Cock-a-doodle-doo!

Time for all the animals to wake up!

Chickens clucking

The hens and the chicks are first to be fed.
Black and White Rabbit gives them corn to eat.
Gray Rabbit collects the eggs from the henhouse.

Cluck!
Cluck!

Did You Know?

Hens can lay eggs every day.
Look what eggs are used for:

Animal Families

Rooster

Hen

Chick

Ducks quacking

Brown Rabbit is feeding the ducks.
The fluffy ducklings are swimming in the pond.
Don't fall in the water, Brown Rabbit!

Quack! Quack!

Did You Know?

Ducks have webbed feet to help them swim.

Animal Families

Drake

Duck

Duckling

Cattle moo-ing

The bull and the cow are ready for breakfast.
Here comes Gray Rabbit with some hay for them.
Look who is feeding the new calf!

Moo! Moo!

Did You Know?

Cows eat grass to make milk. Hay is dried grass.

Milk comes out of the cow's udder.

Animal Families

Bull

Cow

Calf

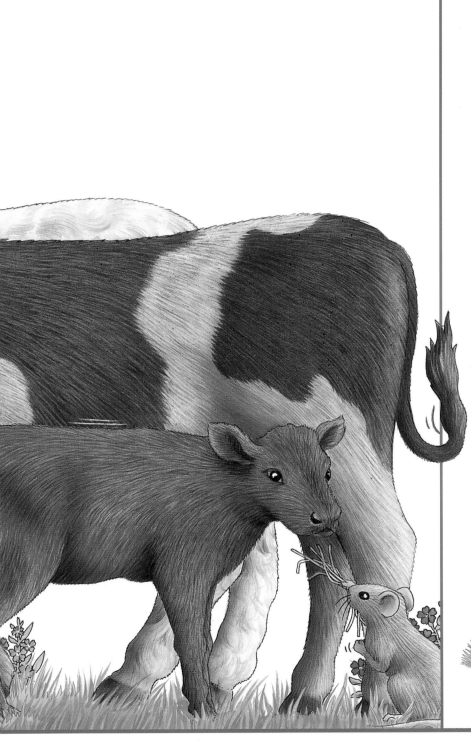

Pigs oinking

The pigs and the piglets are hungry, too.
White Rabbit pours grain into the trough.
The piglets snuggle up to drink their milk.

Oink!
Oink!

Did You Know?

Pigs live in sties. They love to roll around in the mud. Mud protects them from the sun.

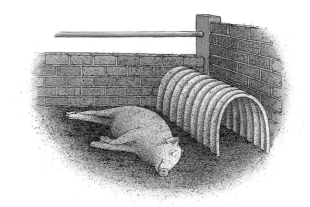

Animal Families

Boar

Sow

Piglet

Sheep baa-ing

Brown Rabbit is taking the sheep to a field where there is a lot of juicy, fresh grass to eat. Hurry up, little lambs!

Baa! Baa!

Did You Know?

Sheep have a woolly coat to keep them warm. Look what else wool is used for:

Animal Families

Ram

Ewe

Lamb

Tractor chugging

It's time to plant the seeds that will grow into wheat.
White Rabbit drives the tractor across the field.
What a lot of noise it makes!

Chug!
Chug!
Chug!

Did You Know?

Tractors pull machines called plows to dig up the ground and make it ready for planting.

Wheat gives us grain, which is made into flour.

FLOUR

Look what flour is used for:

CHIPS

Picking the apples

The apples in the orchard are ready for picking. Some are growing right at the top of the trees. Hold on tight, Black and White Rabbit!

Did You Know?

Lots of different fruits and vegetables are grown on the farm.

Look what apples are used for:

Milking the cows

Now it's time for the cows to be milked.
Brown Rabbit collects the milk in a pail.
Look out for the swishy tail, White Rabbit!

Did You Know?

Cows are milked twice a day on the farm. Most are milked by a special machine.

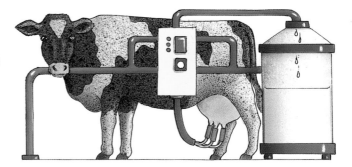

A tanker takes the milk to the factory.

Look what milk is used for:

Let's go shopping

The farm shop sells food that comes from the farm. Black and White Rabbit has a long shopping list. What do you want for dinner, Little Rabbits?

Did You Know?

Most food produced on the farm is taken away by trucks to be sold.

BUNNY'S BEST   FARM FOODS

Look where food is sold:

BUNNY GROCERY

FRUIT & VEG

SUPERMARKET

Goodnight, farm

It's late now, and the Little Rabbits have to go home.
Don't forget to shut the gate behind you!

Zzzz, zzzz!

Goodnight, farm.
Goodnight, Little Rabbits.

Games to play

Playing these games with your child will help them develop observational, verbal, and sorting skills. You will be building their understanding of the world around them and providing the foundation for early literacy and numeracy.

Names and noises

Children love identifying animals and imitating their sounds. Pointing to the pictures, ask your child to name each animal and to make the right animal sound. Alternatively, ask your child to point to the animal whose sound you make. Match the picture of each animal to its label to encourage recognition of these familiar words.

Mix and match

Does the cow live in the henhouse? Does the pig live in the pond? Help your child to match each animal to its farmyard home.

All different kinds

Looking at color, shape, and pattern, help your child describe how the farm animals differ from one another—and in which ways they are similar. How many animals have two legs, and how many have four? Extend and practice vocabulary by providing further detail with words such as fur, feathers, fleece, and tail.

Where's Mouse?

Children adore the game of hide-and-seek. Ask your child to find the little brown mouse that appears throughout the book, and help your child to describe what he is doing.

Food on the farm

Look at the food you have at home, and talk to your child about how this came to be there. Which of the foods described in the book can they find in their refrigerator or cabinets? You may decide to extend this to a discussion about foods not mentioned in the book but familiar to your own child—for example, animal products such as meat.

Day and night on the farm

Try this simple game of spot the difference. Look again at the opening pages and the closing pages of this section. What differences can your child identify between the two scenes? Use this as a basis for a discussion about time—day and night, early and late—and the routines associated with different times of the day.

Little Rabbits'
First
Time
Book

Tick-tock, it's 8 o'clock.

Wake up, Little Rabbits!
It's time for breakfast.
Rise and shine!

Hare Pieces

Welsh Rabbits

BUNNY JOKES ☆

Loads of Bunny

HARE STYLES

It's 8 o'clock.
Move the big hand to the number 12
and the little hand to the number 8.
Use the clocks above to help you!

What time do you wake up?
What do you do before breakfast?

08:00

Tick-tock, it's 9 o'clock.

Time to clean up.
Gray Rabbit is coming
to dinner at 5 o'clock.
Let's get busy!

09:00

It's 9 o'clock.
Move the big hand to the number 12
and the little hand to the number 9.
Use the clocks above to help you!

When do you clean up?
Does cleaning take you a long time
or a short time?

Tick-tock, it's 10 o'clock.

Time to go shopping.
There's a lot to buy at
the supermarket.
Don't forget the carrots!

Carrots
8¢ each

Tomatoes
7¢ each

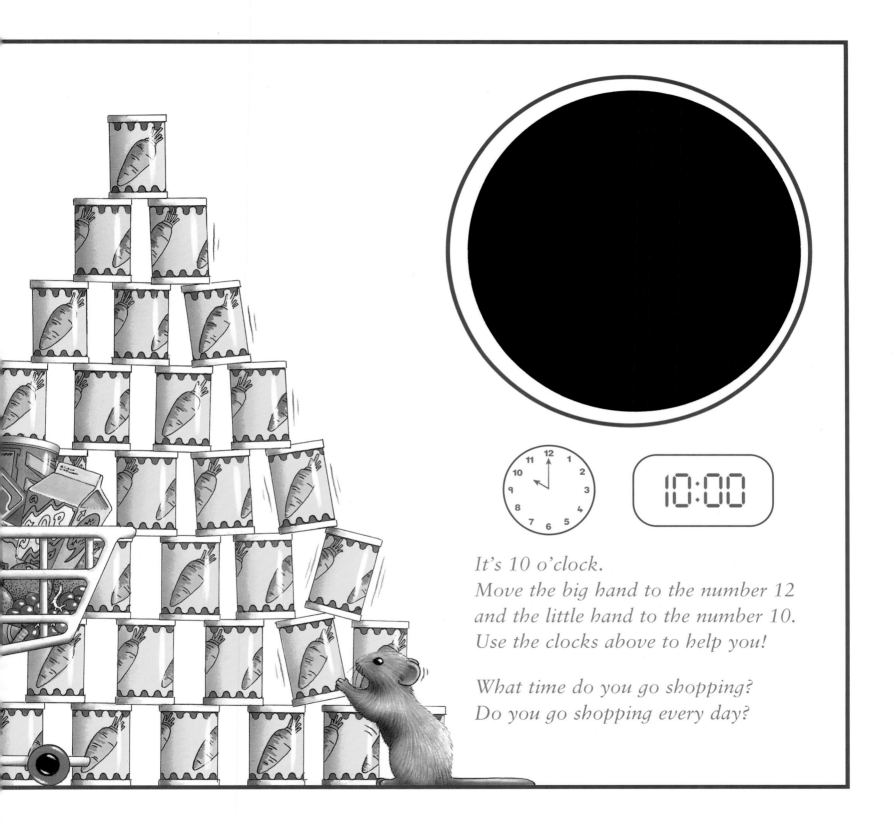

10:00

It's 10 o'clock.
Move the big hand to the number 12
and the little hand to the number 10.
Use the clocks above to help you!

What time do you go shopping?
Do you go shopping every day?

Tick-tock, it's 12 o'clock.

Time for lunch in
the backyard.
And then a little snooze.
Look who's asleep already!

Zzzz, zzzz!

12:00

It's 12 o'clock.
Move the big hand to the number 12
and the little hand to the number 12.
Use the clocks above to help you!

What time do you have lunch?
What do you do after lunch?

Tick-tock, it's 3 o'clock.

Oh, no! Now the Little Rabbits are late. Hurry, hurry, hurry— or dinner won't be ready on time.

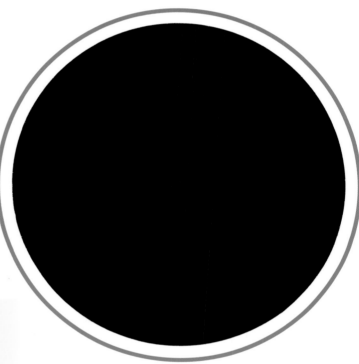

It's 3 o'clock.
Move the big hand to the number 12
and the little hand to the number 3.
Use the clocks above to help you!

Are you sometimes late?
If you are late, do you do things
quickly or slowly?

Tick-tock, it's 5 o'clock.

Gray Rabbit is here.
Hurray, it's time for
dinner…and carrot cake!

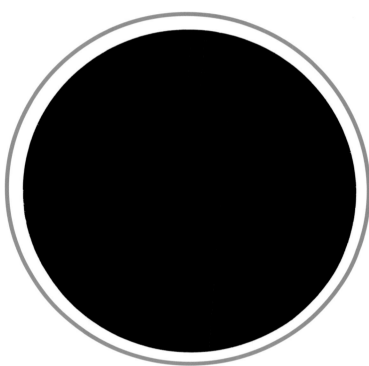

It's 5 o'clock.
Move the big hand to the number 12
and the little hand to the number 5.
Use the clocks above to help you!

What time do you have dinner?
Do you have dinner at the
same time every day?

Tick-tock, it's 7 o'clock.

Time to say good-bye.
What a busy day!
Soon it will be bedtime.

Good night, Little Rabbits,
good night.

RAB 123